Building Community

Practical ways to build inclusive communities for people who are vulnerable

Cara Milne

Building Community

Editing by Jaime Miller of Tascan Consulting Inc.
Cover design by Nikki Takahashi of Fetching Finn Inc.
Author photograph by www.illusionsphotographic.com
Printed in Canada

Milne, Cara, 1976-, author
Building community! : practical ways to build inclusive communities for people who are vulnerable / Cara Milne.

ISBN 978-0-9958316-0-5 (softcover)

1. Community life. 2. Community development. 3. Social integration. 4. People with disabilities. I. Title.

HM761 M55 2017 307 C2016-907800-0

Dedicated to the people with disabilities and their families that I have had the honour to journey alongside. Thank you!

To my beautiful girls, may you both have a lifetime of amazing communities.

Contents

Preface

It was never my intention to write a book. I am known as a talker, not a writer! I have struggled with how to share my work in a written format; however, over the years I have had requests to create a book, and so I started this journey under the premise of writing a simple training manual. I'm not sure why that seemed less scary—but luckily, as my thoughts started flowing, this book eventually transpired. I hope that this collection of ideas, examples, and thoughts will challenge you to envision what it really means to live and participate in an inclusive community.

I am fascinated by and passionate about how we build community for everyone, including those individuals for whom connection may not come naturally. When people ask me what I do for work, I usually respond that I am a community builder for people who are vulnerable. Often that stops the conversation cold. Then I say I am a public speaker. Dead silence. After all these years, I guess this book is finally the explanation of what I really do for a living.

My work has taken me on a variety of adventures. I have supported families, helped young adults to find employment, and aided people who were vulnerable to find their own voice. However, the majority of my work has been teaching. Basically, I have made a career out of talking! I spent many wonderful years instructing at a post-secondary level, and then I fell into this job of public speaking. It was never my plan to have my own company or to travel and speak full time, but that is where life has led me for over fifteen years.

Chances are that you have picked up this book because you have seen my work in person—I love what I do!

People have commented that my work is relevant for everyone, and I appreciate that thought. However, my lens has always been from the perspective of someone with a developmental disability. How do we help someone who is unable to connect easily to others? How do paid staff play a role in helping someone make friends? How do we begin to build up someone's self-esteem in a genuine way? And why do we work so hard just so someone can wave to their neighbour?

I hope that the stories and questions within these chapters will reflect a lifetime of passionate conversations. In the end this book has come from all of you, from the real daily adventures and thoughts that you have shared with me as I travelled and spoke. This book has nine chapters, each with its own theme and follow-up questions. I encourage you to use these questions during your team and family meetings.

Remember, change does not have to be large to be powerful. It is the small daily events that make up what it means to live in community. The simple fact is that we are better when we all belong!

Chapter 1
What are the right words?

Everything you do can either build up or break down stereotypes.
—Cara Milne

Chapter 1

WHAT ARE THE RIGHT WORDS?

Language affects people! It is not just a disability issue. However, when we support individuals with developmental disabilities, the fact is that everything we say or do can either build up stereotypes or break them down. We represent people in our words and attitude, so it is important we are aware of the images we portray.

What we say matters

So, let's start with words. Dr. Maya Angelou (2011) stated that "words are things. . . They get on the walls. They get in your wallpaper. They get in your rugs, in your upholstery, and your clothes, and finally into you." Imagine what a lifetime of hateful words physically looks like. People are burdened by the language that disrespects their worth.

People should always be first, and descriptive language second. So, we want to talk about **people with disabilities**, not "disabled people". John who has autism. Riley who has Down syndrome. Kate who uses a wheelchair (Snow 2008). Why? Does it really matter?

Yes it does! When we refer to people first, we create an attitude of seeing that person before any label or need. When we don't talk about people first, we can get caught up using terms like "the autistic", the "Down's kid" or "the chair". It happens so quickly and often when we try to shorten phrases. When we stop talking about John, Riley, and Kate, we lose the focus and value of whom we are talking about.

I remember hearing a story about Edward, who was getting off an accessible bus. The driver turned to the staff waiting to help Edward and asked, "Are you his handler?" Imagine if that was your son being referred to as an animal. We must recognize the power that comes from words.

What about older terms like calling people *"retarded"* and *"handicapped"?* Quite simply, they've had their time. It is no longer. When you have the honour of representing people, it is important to use language that is current and respectful. Simple. It is part of the responsibility of supporting individuals who are devalued. If changing the terms and words I use helps someone else escape from feeling powerless and insignificant, then I will learn and change as leaders in the disability field encourage it.

I met a family who shared how their son Jeremy was referred to as "the tubie" at school because he was nourished with a feeding tube. I also have a friend whose daughter is regularly called "the chair" because she uses a wheelchair. Such pain comes from casual slogans and nicknames.

What about referring to something (not someone) as "retarded"? The fact is that if you are reading this book, you either work in the field, have a personal connection to someone with a disability, or just want to learn. So I will gently say—it is never okay. It is essential that we talk about **people first and any kind of need or disability second.** Your words can injure people. You are an example to others. Society is listening to how we talk and will copy us.

What we do matters

Let's face it, having the correct language is not enough. Our actions can speak louder than our words. When you sit with your back to a person and look at your phone for hours, it shows that you think this person has nothing to offer.

I walked into a public library one time and heard a really loud voice. I turned a corner and saw a man and his female support staff member. She was on the phone, talking about him and some of his very personal health problems. The entire library could hear it. I felt sick and so, yes, I said something quietly about the fact that everyone could hear her. The staff member was angry with me and said something about "doing" community inclusion.

I am always sad when people use inclusive practice as a weapon. Sure, you were supporting someone to use the library, but your attitude shows me you don't respect or see that person as valuable, and don't care what stereotypes you are building. Sorry, but that is not community building.

Making sure that your attitude shows respect and interest in the person with a disability is important. This includes your clothes. What? Do I need a dress code? No, but consider what happens when people wear nursing scrubs to support individuals with developmental disabilities. They might be comfortable, but they portray an image of someone who is a nurse or someone who is taking care of people who are sick. That is not a stereotype we want to build. Words, body language, and appearances are strong communicators.

Tone of voice is another area to consider. When I talk in a childlike tone of voice, I am building on an existent stereotype of people with disabilities being childlike. We need to see people as their **actual chronological age**. Staff will often come to me and discuss an individual's mental age. I encourage you to keep in mind that although they may have parts of their brain that are not developed typically, they are still twenty or fifty years old. Support is needed, but that doesn't mean we disrespect people's true lived experiences.

> I have seen such extreme differences in attitude regarding how people can be treated because of their age. I remember two different women, Amy and Becky, who were about the same age and had similar disabilities. One organization saw Amy as twenty-two years old; along with receiving twenty-four-hour support, she also wore cool clothes, had pink streaks in her hair, had posters of celebrities on her wall, and volunteered with support. Just down the street was another organization who supported Becky. She was twenty-three years old, but was talked to and treated like a baby. There was juvenile decor in her room, only cartoons on her television, and a focus on physical care. No expectations. Both women needed the same support, but Amy's team respected her twenty-two years of experience. Respect. It just comes down to that.

Educating one person at a time

My experience has been that people don't intend to be offensive; they may just not know better. They may use language that they learned as children. They may have never met anyone with a disability. So, we gently educate one member of the public at a time. A simple correction of a word often works. As an example, when someone says, "I hear you work with *handicapped people*—you must be so patient," I answer, "Yes, I get to work with **people with disabilities** and I love my job." Frequently, folks will quickly realize what they have said and try to copy. At other times, we need to be more specific in how we educate. We may need to calmly explain that using the word "handicapped" is really outdated, but referring to people with disabilities is much more acceptable.

My family has always supported my work in community building, but my parents never really had any connection to someone with a disability. Many years ago, my mother told me a story about a man at her gym. Knowing that certain terms were inappropriate, she paused, careful not to use the word "retarded", and said that he was "mongoloid". My heart sank. Really? (Mongoloid is a very outdated word for Down syndrome—please never use it). The next thing I thought was that if people ever heard her say this and knew she was my mom, I would never work in this field again! I impatiently said, "Mom, the man has Down syndrome. Mongoloid is a very offensive term!" She instantly apologized, and I knew she meant it. She shared how so many terms had changed within her lifetime, and she was never sure which one was correct. I get it! She now uses more current respectful language. For people in your own lives, it may take longer. Don't give up. Now my mother is educating others and is very aware! Go, Mom!

That last story may be a somewhat entertaining example about language, but it is actually about much more than that. People in the community often use respectful words when they are **directly connected** to someone with a disability through their work, school, or neighbourhoods. For example, the more the members of my own family connect directly with people with disabilities, the more they will have a chance to see the individual beyond the stereotype. (Until that happens they are just afraid I will use them in a public example!)

The next chapter will look at the power of really being connected and the implication of what happens when we all truly belong.

Chapter 1 Let's apply this

WHAT ARE THE RIGHT WORDS?

1. What are three things you will take away from reading this chapter? What can you apply right now?

2. Invite families or individuals within your organizations to share some of the painful words/phrases that they have been called. Where have they seen negative attitudes? Be respectful of the stories that you hear.

3. What are some of the disrespectful terms staff have heard or even used? How do you begin to educate? Discuss within your teams and families.

4. What is the current language used in your work place or family to refer to people with disabilities? Is there anything that could be improved?

5. Remember that support teams often represent the arms, legs, and voices for people who are vulnerable! How could your team continue to break down the stereotypes of the people you support?

Chapter 2
What does it really mean to belong?

Inclusion is not a sacrifice of what is best for the individual person. It is a mindset of aiming to support people to have a chance to build community in all circumstances of their daily life.

—Cara Milne

Chapter 2

WHAT DOES IT REALLY MEAN TO BELONG?

In the disability field we have created labels for how we provide services and support for people. We categorize services as **inclusive**, but what does that actually mean? Unfortunately, we have got caught up in terms and lost the actual meaning behind how we support people.

If you were to attend one of my sessions, you would see that I often start by giving my own basic definitions of segregation, integration, and inclusion.

- **Segregation** is when I am grouped together with people who have similar labels as me.

- **Integration** is when I am physically in a space but don't have a chance to be part of the social community.

- **Inclusion** is when I am not only in the physical space but also have a chance to be a part of the social community.

So here is the big question: Which one would feel the loneliest? If you guessed integration, you are right! Being in a space but not having a chance, for example, to play with the other kids at recess, or eat lunch with co-workers, is extremely lonely. There is a big difference between **being tolerated and being accepted.** Integration is being nameless or invisible.

We can call a scenario “inclusive”, but that doesn’t mean a person genuinely belongs.

I remember a mom telling a story about how she and her husband met with the principal of their son’s school. They had been told that their grade 2 son was not allowed to attend his own Easter concert because he would be too “disruptive”. The parents were devastated and were trying to explain to the principal that they would be available for their son during the event, if he needed to leave. They just wanted to **try**! The principal got very angry and yelled, “Your son has inclusion, what else do you want me to do?”

Oh, I had ideas of what I would have liked that principal to do! My call is that the school just thought its only job was to put the child physically in the classroom. However, that is just the beginning of the hard work. Helping this boy connect with kids at recess, eat with peers at lunch, and work on adapted and related school subjects is where the real, hard work comes in.

Inclusion is not about being perfect, but about giving people a chance to have the social connection they are designed for.

In the end the family switched schools. They needed to be in a place which gave them hope that their son could actually be a valued member of a classroom.

What are some examples of inclusive experiences?

There is a big difference between just being physically present and being included. Often staff feel that they have accomplished “inclusion” because the person they are supporting is employed at a job. That is not inclusion.

Inclusion happens when that person is respected and valued while working, is invited to the work Christmas party, and eats lunch with co-workers.

Another example of inclusion is when a child with a disability doesn't just attend Brownies, but has to achieve the same badges, sell cookies, and participate at all the meetings. This little girl may need help and may struggle to know all the words to the Brownie Promise. However, inclusive practice is not about perfection. It is about having **the opportunity to participate** (with or without support) to the best of someone's ability. Just being in a space does not mean we are included. Being included means the person is involved somehow, has a connection with someone, or has responsibility for something.

It is important to acknowledge that not everyone has an easy time being included. For many, it will take a lifetime of effort and creativity. The focus should not be about everyone being included in every single circumstance, but instead always having the chance.

Even people without disabilities are "integrated" for short periods of time. New job, new neighbourhood, or new school—we all start out as guests in these situations. However, individuals with disabilities shouldn't have these feelings of isolation last the entire school year or, worse, a lifetime.

Inclusion is not a sacrifice of what is best for the individual person. It is a mindset of aiming to support people to have a chance to build community in all circumstances of their daily life.

A mom shared a story about how her son Andrew (in grade 5) was struggling with music in school. His class was learning the recorder and the sounds were causing this little boy great distress (I have no doubt the recorder has caused many ears great distress). The mom asked that her son go only for a few minutes to music class and then, when it got too loud, head to the library to read. When the teacher was asked about this, he said "No, because that is not inclusion."

This story always makes me sad. I appreciate a teacher who wants to help this little boy be included. Yet, we must really look at what the child needs. Having Andrew excuse himself for twenty minutes would not create the social barriers that crying and yelling in music class would.

But wait! What about segregated options?

This is a hard but important question. People frequently misunderstand segregated experiences. Segregation is not isolation! Segregation has community—it just happens to be with people who have similar labels. Repeatedly we discredit the possible community that can occur within segregated experiences.

Although I did not have much experience with Special Olympics, I had the opportunity to attend a variety of track and field events one year. (I was dating the head coach and ended up marrying him!) I had some preconceived ideas that people with disabilities would be lonely and not want to be part of these segregated sporting events. However, over time I met athletes, coaches, and families and I saw something I hadn't expected. Community! Yes, people felt they belonged. They were part of something bigger and felt valued.

To be clear—just because people have a disability does not mean they always want to be a part of a segregated class or event. The key is that all experiences are specific to who the people are and what they are looking for. I fear that people will discredit the possibility of community because it doesn't have the proper label. Every so often in my workshops, I draw a simple chart like the one below and ask the groups to insert a phrase that would describe the different experiences. I am not asking which one is better, but what each one may feel like.

Isolation	**Segregation**	**Integration**	**Inclusion**
I am lonely	I belong with a specific group	I am a guest	I belong

There is no perfect formula for supporting people. We simply need to be aware of what is occurring at different parts of the day and understand what is working and what is not. I hope that support teams and families will take a bigger look at all the different opportunities for community and make sure that people are not guests in their own life.

I was visiting with a team who supported John, a funny and charming thirty-five-year-old man with a developmental disability. I was asked to help him with building his community. We discussed what was on his existing calendar and saw that it was pretty blank. He was lonely. When I asked what he used to enjoy doing, he mentioned going to a dance. It turns out there is a monthly dance for people with disabilities in his area. When I asked why he wasn't going—when all his friends where there—he told me that the staff wouldn't take him to anything segregated. He said that the staff told him he didn't belong there.

What have we done? We support individuals who are devalued and then isolate them even further by determining whom they are "allowed" to visit with, based on social labels. If John were not enjoying the dances, then of course he shouldn't be going. However, in this case and in so many circumstances I have seen, support teams are the ones who create the social boundaries and isolation for people.

After a long meeting, we created a list of events and quality things that John could be involved in. (As a hint, they were not one-time events. So often that is not the solution to building community.) The list included mowing some of his neighbours' lawns, lifting weights at his local gym, and **yes**, stopping by the monthly dance. The support team made a deal that he could go and if it wasn't fun, someone would come and get him right away. We must stop creating extra barriers for people who already fight so hard to belong.

Wait! Is only segregation okay?

Am I saying that only having segregated activities is okay? Great question! Yes, there is community within segregation; unfortunately, something really critical is lost when only people with disabilities are grouped together. The community misses out!

If there are only segregated classrooms, then my girls would miss out on getting to know someone with a disability in their class. It is the rest of the community that misses out on getting to know, and having relationships with someone who has a disability.

Remember the story about my mom in Chapter 1? I have repeatedly reflected on the fact that, although she is interested in learning language that is current and appropriate, it won't be until she actually has a relationship with someone with a disability that her reasons for doing so will change. For now she wants to please me and not be offensive to others because she is a great person. However, if one day she has a neighbour with Down syndrome and they become friends, she will experience a deeper attitude shift.

Where do we start?

On this complicated adventure, consider building opportunities in the community by looking for the natural, community-based option first.

Remember, we can still support specialized, segregated events. We never want to take anything away from people, but only to build upon what opportunities are already in place. However, if we do not discuss the possibility of generic, public-based options, staff with good intentions invariably begin by going to segregated activities.

For example, if I am supporting TJ, and he is interested in photography, I may instinctively enrol him in a "special" photography class at the agency. This may be an amazing class, but could we just slow down and check first if there is a community photography class available near where TJ lives? He may need support there, but we should take the time to try community options first.

One simple illustration of this is when Zac wanted to become physically healthier. His support team not only helped him purchase a gym membership at a local gym, but also arranged for an orientation that fit his skill set. It would have been easier to have Zac work out at the agency where he was supported, but instead they started with a local option. Awesome!

In the end, the gym was eager to learn how to make Zac's experience a positive one. Sometimes the community really does say yes! Zac is now improving his health and expanding his own community. He feels like he belongs!

In summary, it is important to realize that one person could naturally have many different experiences in one day. I can live with roommates who also have disabilities, and share a chat and coffee together with them in the morning. I can then go on the bus, where the driver knows my name. I can go to work, where my co-workers wave good morning and ask me how my night was. I can be invited to a birthday party and have a blast, and so on. Just keep in mind that it is a journey. We just need to take one step at a time; one opportunity at a time.

Chapter 2 Let's apply this

WHAT DOES IT REALLY MEAN TO BELONG?

1. What are three things you will take away from reading this chapter? What can you apply right now?

2. a. Look at the different events of people's day, week, and month, and areas of school, work, home, or play. When do people feel like they belong?

   b. When do they feel like a guest? When do they feel lonely?

3. How can you celebrate the stories that demonstrate people being a genuine part of their communities?

4. Where can you begin to explore community connections for the people who are vulnerable you care about? Remember to check out what the community offers!

Chapter 3
Are we aiming towards inclusive practice?

Community is where you are noticed, known, and missed.
—Cara Milne

Chapter 3

ARE WE AIMING TOWARDS INCLUSIVE PRACTICE?

Being included means people notice us, they wave hello, and we have eye contact. Often staff and families look for large-scale "inclusive practice" signs, like a job or membership card. However, the simplest acts show us that we are included: a welcoming smile or the fact that someone knows our name. Better yet, is the person missed? If they are absent for a while, does anyone notice?

Being noticed, known, and missed

Being noticed, known, and missed are three simple but powerful ways to look at what it means to belong. Some of you might be reflecting on the fact that this already happens in the lives of some of the people you support. Yes! Unfortunately, we are not always acknowledging this success.

Being noticed, known, and missed is important not just for individuals who are vulnerable. According to Susan Pinker (2014), people have a universal hunger to connect and belong. We are happier, healthier, and more resistant to disease and despair if we satisfy the need for meaningful human contact. Our loads seem lighter; the hills are less steep. Genuine social interaction is a force of nature we all need.

Of all the different topics I speak about, often "noticed, known, and missed" is the one everyone remembers. It reminds people that we frequently have community right in front of us, but we don't see it.

Someone told me a story about Adam, who regularly went to the bank on his own. One day Adam went to the bank, but the cashiers there soon realized that Adam was not himself. After he left, one cashier took the time to contact the organization supporting Adam and shared her concern. When the support staff checked on him back at home, they realized his blood sugars were way off and took him to the hospital. The bank teller possibly saved Adam's life. This did not happen because Adam went to that bank once. It happened because Adam was **known** there.

I have heard so many stories from staff who say something like, "I just realized that when John walks into the 7-Eleven, everyone says hello and knows his name. They ask how he is!" Celebrate this! Here are a few more scenarios to watch for:

- A neighbour waving hello! Excellent—now, who is waving back?

- A clerk at a familiar store smiling and looking at someone in the face. Frequently the community looks away when people with disabilities enter a store or walk down the street. Be aware of who is actually looking at John in the face, with a smile. These small but significant moments matter.

- A co-worker inviting someone to work events (potlucks, birthday lunches, Christmas parties).

- A classmate giving high-fives in the hall on the way to class.

- An acquaintance asking support staff the amazing question, "I haven't seen Amy in a while. Is she okay?"

- My roommate greeting hello when I walk in the door.

What are some other examples of inclusive experiences? There is a big difference between being physically there and being included. Staff may believe they have achieved inclusion because the person they are supporting is hanging around the mall. Instead, inclusion occurs when the person is walking at the mall while other people typically "walk" the mall (before the malls open), and that person is known by the other mall walkers. Or it means that the child doesn't just attend school but has opportunities to play with other children at recess, learn the same subjects, and has responsibilities within the classroom.

Remember just being in a space does not mean we are included there. We need to be involved in something, have a connection with someone, or have responsibilities.

I fear that we are not celebrating and recognizing the simple but meaningful connections that people have. Support teams need to slow down. Look around and be aware of existing opportunities. I challenge all organizations to really look for (and then celebrate) when people see someone they know and wave hello!

I recently attended an awards ceremony where a self-advocate received an award for the steps he had taken to make his own life and the life of his community better. This gentleman shared how his current employer had made such a big impact on his life. He said, "I love my job because they **see me** there." Powerful words! He literally felt noticed!

Safety

Being noticed, known, and missed is more than just acknowledging and celebrating community. It has another very important function. **We are safer!** This is why I want my girls to be known on our street when they play outside. Keeping people who are vulnerable safe should be a constant priority. However, safety does not derive from isolation. Instead, when staff study abuse prevention (Government of Alberta 2016), they see that an important component is helping people be involved in their communities, where others can get to know them!

Take the time to reflect on this. How are people safer when more of the public knows who they are? Their routines? Their interests and fears?

A team shared a story with me about Rick, a gentleman they supported, who left the house without them knowing. He literally crawled out the front door and down the street. Staff didn't know he could even open the door! The next-door neighbour saw Rick crawling down the sidewalk and realized something was wrong, but didn't know who the man was or where he lived. So, the neighbour called the police

After an afternoon of paperwork and stress, the staff

reflected that had the neighbour known Rick, recognized him, and knew where he lived, he would have been safer.

DOORS—a helpful tool

After having so many conversations about how to view community building, I created a simple acronym to help teams examine whether situations lead to belonging or loneliness. I hope you will use DOORS in your own work and support teams.

D:	**Dignity**
O:	**Opportunity for relationships**
O:	**Opportunity for community**
R:	**Responsibility**
S:	**Self-esteem**

D Does the person have dignity, privacy, and respect for their actual age?

O Does the person have an opportunity for relationships? We cannot make friends for people, but we can create situations and support skills that offer the individual a **chance** to make friends.

O Does the person have an opportunity for community? Are they noticed, known, and missed?

R Does the person have responsibility? What is he or she in charge of? See Chapter 6 for more information.

S Does the person have positive self-esteem?

The DOORS acronym is a way to examine services and supports. Services might be called inclusive, but if people feel terrible about themselves, are treated like children, and are lonely, something about those services needs to shift. What matters is not what we label a service, but what is actually happening!

Finding purpose with positive roles

All people need to have purpose in their day. Often individuals with disabilities have days that are filled with activities. They are passing the time doing nice things, but they are not genuinely involved in anything, have no responsibility, and repeatedly have no connection with anyone around them.

Swimming is an example that may be helpful. There is nothing wrong with occasionally going to Open Swim to get some exercise and enjoy the pool. However, that is just an activity. Activities are certainly a part of everyone's week, but they are not everything.

On the other hand, when we see people as "swimmers", then we start to search for genuine swimming experiences. Swimmers would be people who join an Aquasize class, and after some time a few people in the group smile and say hello when they enter the pool. Swimmers read about swimming in the sports headlines. They watch it on television. It is a part of their identity.

There is a very big difference between roles and activities. **Roles are about identity** and how we see ourselves. They are the reason behind why we do things.

Kristin's goal was to become more independent at home. The team that supported her wanted to focus on building positive roles, not just keeping her busy. So, after attending my training session, they simply started with listing the activities she was already doing. Then they shifted their effort to helping her focus on a positive role (as a daughter) rather than activities (cleaning the house and cooking).

So, Kristin was supported in the **role** of daughter, and she invited her parents to come over. She then got groceries, planned the meal, baked, vacuumed and dusted the house, and wore something nice.

The muffins didn't turn out (and that is okay!), but the staff couldn't believe the difference in Kristin and the success of the week. Roles bring purpose to any activities. It is the reason we do things.

I have witnessed "vacuuming programs", and yet those people vacuuming have never had anyone over to visit in their home. I have seen people kept busy by colouring, but never acknowledged as artists. There are individuals who learn "baking skills" but then the baked items are thrown out. Purpose has been lost. To be clear, it is okay that when I bake, I end up burning the cookies. Roles are not about mastery but identity.

When we see people as hosts, daughters, cooks, gardeners, sports fans, and friends, we can support creative and purpose-filled days. There is no magic formula for community building. For some people the path is long and the improvements small. However, if we continue to have a vision of what belonging in community looks like, we can head in the right direction.

Chapter 3 Let's apply this

ARE WE ARE AIMING TOWARDS INCLUSIVE PRACTICE?

1. What are three things you will take away from reading this chapter? What can you apply right now?

2. How are the people you support noticed, known, and missed? Make a specific list with names of people.
   Look over the list to see how many are **not** paid to be in a person's life. Make small steps to ensure that all these relationships are supported.

3. In what ways does your organization tell monthly stories/reports of how people are noticed, known, and missed in the community? Remember that this process needs to be ongoing within organizations and support teams.

4. What are the current positive roles for people you support? What are their hobbies and interests? Are they a family member? Employee? Volunteer? Other?

5. What is one area where you need to increase the feeling of community for yourself?

Chapter 4
Where is the community?

Community is actually right where you are! It is not something you can leave and then go back to.
It is where you journey, it is the path you walk. It is at home, on the bus, at work, at school, at a coffee shop or walking home.
It is the people around you, wherever your day leads.

—Cara Milne

Chapter 4

WHERE IS THE COMMUNITY?

Where is the community? I love this question. I think we can get caught talking about "getting out" in the community or "community building" without a good definition of what that really means. Let's look at one of my favourite stories that provides a good start for us to define community.

When traveling for my work, I often get invited to share meals with people. (Okay, yes, it may be that sometimes I invite myself, but that is a different book.) One evening I was eating with three gentlemen who had developmental disabilities, along with their support team. Over the course of my travels, I had got to know these men fairly well. As we were eating, they were sharing stories about their life. There was teasing, laughter, and an overall wonderful atmosphere in the home. After dinner, coffee was poured and we started to eat the dessert I had brought. I remember thinking how proud I was of the work that was happening in this house. It is not an easy thing to create an environment that feels comfortable and safe; it takes great effort and an attention to important details.

Suddenly, one of the staff jumped up, looked at her watch, and said, "John, it is time to go, it is your community inclusion time!" There was silence. I asked where they were going and was told that three times a week John and his staff go out for coffee. (Interesting, I thought, as we are **already** drinking coffee). "Are you meeting anyone there?" I asked. No, it was just going to be this support staff and John.

If you know me, you can guess that I was trying really hard not be a consultant and wanted to remain an invited guest. But I couldn't help wondering, "Why are they leaving?" After all, we were having such a fun night, and I could tell John was having a blast!

John, in his own way, shared that he was not interested in going, and (thankfully) the intuitive staff heard his request. But the moment really stuck with me. After the dishes were done, I gently asked the staff member why she felt the need to still stick with the schedule when John was obviously having such a wonderful evening. She was honest and answered, "I have to take John out into the community three times a week. I have an 'inclusion chart' that I must fill in. I know he was enjoying himself, but we are evaluated based on how often we get people out in public."

I loved this young woman. She was honest, insightful, and frustrated. Here is the answer I gave her, and the one I continue to share everyday: home is community too! **Community is actually right where you are.** It is not something you can leave and then go back to. It is where you journey, it is the path you walk. It is at home, on the bus, at work, at school, at a coffee shop, or walking home. It is the people around you, wherever your day leads.

Community is everywhere!

So, if we are going to define community, let's start by recognizing that community is right where you are! You cannot create it, but you can be aware of it and embrace it. Be aware of who is around you at all times. I find that as an industry, we have overlooked the importance of home, thinking that it doesn't count as community. Many support staff consider walking out the front door towards something as a "community outing", but I challenge you to remember that the front door also opens to let people in! Who is coming over for a visit?

Community is having meaningful relationships with people and includes places that exist within and outside the service system. More specifically, when you support someone to go to a public event but walk right by a friendly neighbour without stopping to chat, you are missing an opportunity. Slow down and look for simple, small opportunities to build connection for the people you care about.

We have overlooked the importance of the bus ride, the casual conversation at the coffee shop with the barista, or the chat with the sales clerk. Community is right where you journey, and I challenge support teams and families to slow down. Recognize the gems that are already there. Where can the person be noticed, known, and missed?

But what happens when the community says no?

One barrier to this idea is when the community disrespects people with disabilities. What if the person on the bus gives John a dirty look, or the cashier ignores him, or the neighbour petitions to not have a "group home" on the street? It is heartbreaking when the community says no and forfeits the chance to connect and include someone with a disability.

However, not everyone is disrespectful to people who are vulnerable. There may be a nasty, unfriendly neighbour but there is often a wonderful one too. Someone on the bus may be disrespectful, but the bus driver may be friendly. When supporting individuals who are devalued, we must continue to focus on the positive connections and not let the negative interactions prohibit possibilities. Building community for people with disabilities can be hard, and even tiny steps forward need to be celebrated.

A support staff recently told me a story of her visit to a coffee shop with Helen, whom she was supporting. After they sat down to enjoy their coffee, two older gentlemen loudly remarked that "she" should not be there but back in an institution. Heartbreaking to hear and painful to experience. A different person sitting in the coffee shop heard the horrible comment and ended up coming to sit with Helen and her staff. The newcomer loudly exclaimed how happy she was to meet Helen and how Helen shouldn't worry about what those cranky old men said. I wish we could always have such an advocate in every coffee shop!

Why does the community say no?

Often it is ignorance. It comes when people don't have a personal connection to someone with a disability. Stereotypes have overshadowed the actual person. How do we fight that? Honestly, I think it is one relationship at a time. We need to look for any chance for the person to be seen and their skills or abilities to be noticed. It is a daily effort to breakdown stereotypes and build up personhood.

I worked alongside a support home that had a huge renovation. When it was all done, the organization had a great idea to host an open house and invite their direct neighbours. What a great way to invite the community in! One neighbour stopped by and exclaimed, "Wow, it is so clean," stayed for ten minutes, and left. The staff were not sure what to think of his comment, but after debriefing realized that his stereotypes of a supported home were rapidly changing and that the open house was worth it. This neighbour is not best friends with the people who live in the home, but he does wave every time he sees them and knows everyone's name. That is progress and worthy of celebration. Barriers are broken one personal connection at a time.

How do we repair situations when things go wrong?

When we really start supporting people to connect to their communities, things can also go wrong. People will accidently get lost, lose things, cause disruption, or get upset. It is not always easy. It is important to not give up because something went awry.

However, part of helping people connect and stay connected is repairing relationships and situations when something has gone wrong. First, start with an apology. Express regret to the store owner for the mess or apologize to the neighbour for someone yelling too loud late at night. Just acknowledging the concerning behaviour or incident can often begin the healing of a tentative relationship.

Second, educate. Help bring the stereotypes down by explaining why people react the way they do. Is it past experiences? Is it how their brain works? Just explain it in basic ways, but with more information than a label. For example, it doesn't help the store owner when I say, "Sorry he is yelling. He has autism." Instead, try, "Sorry John is yelling. He has autism and it is loud in here; that is hard for him, yet he loves your store. So, we are going to take a walk outside."

One of my favourite stories of all time relates to this topic. An agency was supporting Lisa to attend a local Aquasize class. Lisa's attendance in the class was going amazingly well and the team realized that Lisa didn't need support to attend, so they backed off! They no longer attended with her, but did stop by occasionally to check on her. Perfect! Unforgettably, one day a staff person named Karen stopped by, and there was Lisa totally naked in the pool!

Yes. Some days will be like this. We support complex and interesting people. So . . . what do we do? My gentle answer is that we need to repair this situation. This is how Karen handled it:

The first thing was to deal with the crisis. Karen got Lisa out of the pool and Lisa put some clothes on. Karen and Lisa apologized to the teacher. Lisa then apologized to the other women in the pool. Karen not only apologized though, she also educated along the way. She explained that Lisa loved the class and didn't mean to offend or embarrass anyone. She grew up in an institutional setting and was never taught privacy. Unfortunately, for that specific class Lisa simply forgot her bathing suit and didn't see the harm in being naked alongside other women. We all have reasons for behaviour.

The following week Karen and her team continued to find ways to repair these relationships. They ended up baking cookies and Lisa handed them out during the next class. They were not just regular cookies; these were gingerbread men decorated to look like naked women! Awesome!

There are so many ways to repair relationships. I know of a home that helped Devin write a note of apology when he kicked down a board on a neighbour's fence. Devin wasn't angry at that neighbour, and this was part of the explanation. Devin delivered the personalized note with some baking (food always helps). The staff felt that it helped relieve some of the tension and stereotypes between Devin and his neighbour. Devin of course also fixed the fence!

Be creative around restoring relationships with the general public. Don't give up just because of one bad incident. Fight to repair it! Continue to wave, to smile, and to look for opportunities for community building.

Chapter 4 Let's apply this

WHERE IS THE COMMUNITY?

1. What are three things you will take away from reading this chapter? What can you apply right now?

2. What are specific situations or areas that you feel are working to build community for people you care about? How can you protect and celebrate those?

3. If community is right where you are, then what opportunities have you missed?

4. a. What are some examples of a personal connection that someone you support has made (other than with people who are paid)?

   b. What are the next steps to supporting these relationships even further?

Chapter 5
Is home community too?

People will live in homes they hate because of neighbourhoods they love, and people will move from homes they love because of neighbourhoods they hate.
It matters!

—*Cara Milne*

Chapter 5

IS HOME COMMUNITY TOO?

I am passionate about celebrating the community-building possibilities of home. It is an underused and under-celebrated area when supporting people who are vulnerable. It is the place we should always begin. Community is at home too!

Valuable moments at home

Unfortunately, support teams often see "day services" as the main chance for people who are vulnerable to connect to people and places around them. Do not discredit the simple but important things that happen in the evening and at home. Watching favourite television shows with friends or roommates, chatting online or on the phone, making and preparing dinner, or learning how to take care of oneself and home are all purposeful activities that can lead to significant opportunities for building community.

When travelling, I occasionally have dinner at the homes where I have working relationships (okay, maybe I invite myself over). When I called one team to make plans, the supervisor said that they would love to have me over, but they did not have any extra kitchen chairs. Um, really? In the most diplomatic way possible, I shared that I was sure they would find an extra chair and I would look forward to being there at six o'clock. Dinner ended up being great, and yes, they found some extra chairs!

I wasn't upset about my own awkward dinner invitation, but I was disappointed to realize that if there was no room for me at the table, there was no room for anyone else either. There were no guests, ever. Six months later, this home ended up buying the largest kitchen table I have ever seen. There is room for you now too!

Sharing meals together

I am currently raising two teenage girls. I feel like that statement needs to be in a book all on its own! However, did you know eating five to seven meals a week as a family can improve a teenager's grades and physiological health? Even if the meal is simple and sometimes strained (Damour 2016). Meals are not about having perfect moments but about sharing life together—having a place and time where people care about me and my day.

Residential services have this natural gift of people sharing meals together. Unfortunately, when supporting people with disabilities, dinnertime has frequently been broken down into tasks in order to get things done as quickly and cleanly as possible. Slow down. Start by looking at who plans all the meals, and make sure that everyone gets a say.

Then aim to have everyone, including staff, sit down and eat together. This idea causes duress for many support teams, often because staff are used to eating separately. I challenge you to try to eat with **everyone together** at least once a month.

The fact is that if staff are eating the meals, they will be much more aware of what they are cooking. I acknowledge that budgets and allergies can become barriers, but be creative and look at ways to get past these obstacles.

I have seen the quickest and largest changes come from just changing how dinnertime works. In one home, Mike, Audrey, Jane, and Scott did not eat together or have any resemblance of fellowship. Staff served everything and then ate different meals at different times. It didn't feel like home and it was not somewhere I would want to spend time.

The support team began with small changes. They started by having Sunday night dinners "family style". They often had simple casseroles that were not expensive and that everyone could eat. The team made an effort to have everyone sit together, including all the staff who were working. They tried to have the food on the table to be dished out, instead of served by staff. Of course, some issues happened, and they told me how Mike once ate the entire bowl of potatoes that was supposed to be for the whole home!

It is not always going to go perfectly, but in the end, it is worth the effort and struggle. Two years later everyone in this home (including staff) eat every dinner meal together. They keep condiments and salad on the table. Audrey now feels it is important that a blessing be said before everyone eats, and everyone in the house respects this. It is a totally different environment, and the four people who live there would love to have you stop by. Dinner is at 5:30 sharp!

In the end, we really must consider what we would want our own lives, or the lives of our children, to be like if the roles were reversed. If I were in an accident and you ended up supporting me, I would want you to knock on my door before entering, acknowledge me when you walk in a room, talk to me, touch me in kindness, look at me, eat with me, and sit with me. Let me be a part of the life of the home, even if that is just me sitting in the kitchen and listening to the chatter of dinner preparations.

Also, don't forget that contribution and responsibility is imperative when supporting people in their homes. Repeatedly, staff do all the tasks because it is quicker and easier, but that doesn't make daily life better. Make sure people don't feel like guests in their own home.

Oh yes—invite people in!

Home is also an excellent place to invite community in! Who is coming by? Who comes for dinner and when? Look for opportunities to host. Birthdays and holidays are great excuses to make sure that doorbell is ringing and there is food to share on the table. It is not about huge or glamourous events; in fact, intimate, short visits are perfect.

I have heard on numerous occasions that support teams don't like to invite people over because roommates get jealous of each other's guests. Sigh. Let's get this straight: when people are lonely and when a visitor comes, everyone is eager to participate and "behaviour" can happen? Please never say that because people are sad when they don't get a visitor, then no one can come! Could we instead look at inviting more people over? Yes, that would take work, but luckily we can start now.

There are homes that require a confidentiality form to be filled out before guests can enter the home. Yikes! Now that screams **barrier**, and I can't think of anything worse than this kind of documentation to build up stereotypes. However, on the flip side, it is imperative that we also help keep people safe. So, I would definitely not recommend inviting over the creepy neighbour. Just start with conversations on the lawn with people who seem interested. Remember, we are safer when we are noticed, known, and missed.

I was meeting with one team who supported Craig and Graham, and the team was talking about the neighbours. One staff member shared how the neighbours on the street were really nosy. "Why do you think that?" I asked. She explained that Graham had needed an ambulance, and once the paramedics left, the neighbour came over, rang the doorbell, and asked if everything was okay!

I don't think that neighbour was nosy. I think that was exactly what we hoped would happen! The team and I chatted about how to handle this kind of opportunity next time. Does that neighbour need to know every medical detail? Of course not! However, you can start by inviting her in and sharing how kind it was that she inquired. Maybe add that in a few days when Graham is better, the team will help him stop by.

I think the fundamental problem is not about doorbells ringing, but about teams seeing people's homes as work sites. When we see homes as just "houses" and places of work, we will never be ready to invite the community in.

Neighbours—my very favourite of all topics

If you have seen my work in person, you know that when I start talking about neighbours, I often get the most animated. Why? It matters! They are an untapped or underused opportunity for community. Guess what—this is not just a disability issue. I have done workshops on neighbourhood building for city employees and different municipalities.

Community building is something that takes work and effort, but can change entire neighbourhoods and communities.

Every so often I have staff in my workshops who become uncomfortable when we start talking about supporting **homes**, not houses. A lovely lady, Brittney, was honest and shared that she doesn't know a single one of her neighbours and doesn't like to host events or even have pictures on her walls. I hear this. I get it is hard to support people in a different way than how you live.

I told Brittney not to worry, that I was not going to track her down in her own home and make her host her neighbours! But it is not about Brittney. It is about the unique people she supports, John and Amy. It is about supporting people who are vulnerable to have an opportunity for community building. It is about keeping John and Amy safer because more people know who they are. In the end, it is a part of Brittney's job. So, just start with a wave. I know you can do it, Brittney!

But this is hard! Yes, sometimes trying to connect with neighbours doesn't work. They are not interested or, worse, they are disrespectful. Don't give up. Keep looking at opportunities for contribution and ways to take down the barriers of stereotypes. Remember that it is not about being best friends with every neighbour. It is, however, about knowing people who live near you and, more importantly, who live near the people you support.

I struggled to pick my favourite story to talk about the importance of neighbours. In the end, I cannot. I have had a lifetime of living near and sharing life with amazing people.

> My husband and I have lived on streets where there was an annual golf tournament with a trophy! We currently live on a street that holds at least two major block parties a year. There is a Facebook page just for the people who live on our street—thirty-seven folks and growing. We have a "book pub" that started out with four people and now has a dozen women who meet regularly. These people have become a foundation for our family, and I am willing to drive all over the city for school and sports just so we can live near them.

We don't necessarily have an exceptional street, but we have intentionally got to know the amazing people who live near us. It is possible for anyone—and for us it has made all the difference.

In the home and surrounding neighbourhood

Building community at home should focus on what is happening both within the home and outside in the neighbourhood. Let's break those two areas down even further. I have included a variety of questions below to help support teams. I have used John for examples of **within** the home and Amy for examples of **outside** the home to help guide us.

What is happening for John within his home?

- Does John have any choice about what he eats? If support teams are looking for a place to start, try Sunday dinners. Then, hey, maybe John could invite someone to join him!

- Does John take part in buying the groceries? This could mean he gets all the groceries or just a few of them. Does he help purchase the food at whatever skill level he can?

- Who does John eat with? I am thinking specifically about dinnertime. Is there a family environment where everyone eats together or does he eat alone? Where is fellowship happening? Does everyone (including staff) eat the same food? What does the atmosphere feel like at dinnertime? Is it the best time of the day or is it just about eating and leaving?

- Are there pictures of John everywhere? Pictures tell a story; use them! Have pictures up on the walls and in public places to help share John's story. I challenge organizations to have two personal pictures up for every one work document on the wall.

- What jobs does John have at home? Yes, contribution is important at home too! What is John responsible for? For example, does he help clean up after dinner?

- Does John have a set of keys for his home?

- Who answers the door? If John can, how do you ensure that he does?

- Who answers the phone? If John is capable, how do you ensure that he does?

- Whose voice is on the answering machine? Just think of the fun in this!

- For what events does John get to be a host in his home?

- Who sets the schedule for the day? Can John be home in the day? If not, how can we look at this possibility?

- Finally, does John feel safe in his home?

What is happening for Amy outside her home and in her neighbourhood?

- Do Amy's neighbours know her name? Do they wave at her and acknowledge her? Is she noticed, known, and missed?

- Does Amy know any of her neighbours' names?

- How does Amy respond to the people around her? If she can't wave, are her support teams representing her and waving?

- Does Amy's house exterior match the other homes in the neighbourhood? Are there flowerpots outside? Is the snow shovelled? Could Amy be a part of gardening and shovelling?

- Does Amy take advantage of social opportunities in her neighbourhood? Block parties, garage sales, and

Halloween are perfect occasions to try to connect with neighbours!

- How does Amy contribute to her neighbourhood? Does she ever host anything? Or take care of someone else's home? How does she make her neighbourhood better?

- Does Amy know the name of the person who delivers the mail or newspaper?

- Do staff parking their cars on the street or driveway cause an angry barrier between Amy and her neighbours? If so, they need to be moved.

- Does Amy feel safe on her street?

You are probably realizing that to have some of these areas be successful, you need to slow down. Interestingly, this chapter was the hardest to write, probably because it is so important for me to get across the remarkable opportunities for building community at home. So just start with inviting someone over for a cup of tea and wave at your neighbours!

Chapter 5 Let's apply this

IS HOME IS COMMUNTY TOO?

1. What are three things you will take away from reading this chapter? What can you apply right now?

2. Celebrate and tell stories of experiences at home and in the neighbourhood that are working.

3. Make a list of the names of the neighbours whom the support team knows. Literally list the names and house numbers. In six months make sure the list is longer.

4. Plan a day for the people you support to host a brunch, coffee, or dinner event. Who is invited? What need to be done to prepare? Enjoy!

5. How could the support team improve eating and sharing meals? What is the next step for your team?

6. When is the next block party or garage sale?

Chapter 6
How do we build up responsibility?

It is not helpful when we do things for people that they could do for themselves. Slow down!
—Cara Milne

Chapter 6

HOW DO WE BUILD UP RESPONSIBILITY?

Staff and families need to keep in mind that their role is to support but not to do everything for someone. "Do with, not for" is a reminder that people should have as much autonomy as possible. What exactly is autonomy? It is having personal independence and the opportunity to make decisions, act on them, and then experience the consequences.

But it's faster when I do it!

It's true—it is likely easier for staff or families if they just do everything! However, that does not mean it is in the best interests of the individuals they care about. When we do things for people that they can do on their own, we are not actually helping them. To clarify, although you will often assist people because of their needs or disabilities, you also need to be aware of what they still **can do** and then support them to maintain and increase those skills.

Sometimes support staff will rush to get someone dressed, and then they have nowhere to go. Or they quickly drive a person to an activity, when they could have taken the city bus. Ask the question "What is the hurry?" and remember that there is value in the process. Do not focus on getting things done, as the journey is just as important as the destination.

We often do everything for people because it is faster and easier (and maybe even cleaner), but in the end, it is not helpful when we take away jobs or responsibilities that people can do themselves. It is important to slow down.

Velcro staff

Have you ever felt like you should be a "bubble" around people you care about? Do you act like the two of you are attached to each other? Be cognizant of this and make sure you are always aware of who else from the community could be a part of the team. Who can you invite in?

Helping people is less about being one-on-one and more about being aware of the opportunity for community. Think of it literally like two pieces of Velcro—it is important that we don't have the pieces touching all the time. Be aware of where space could occur.

On the other hand, yes, you need to help keep people safe and meet their needs. This is not about a lack of support. This is an awareness about where you are physically becoming the barrier to other possible connections. Look around!

Many years ago, my daughter attended a weekly class with a little girl who had a developmental disability. My daughter didn't ever mention the disability; the most she ever said was that Natalie wore glasses. How amazing that children just don't see differences! After some time, my daughter stopped talking about Natalie. When I asked if she played with Natalie anymore, she said, "Oh Mommy, I don't have to play with her anymore. The teacher-lady does it now!"

I still feel heartbroken that this natural opportunity for the two of them ended. Unfortunately, a well-meaning teacher's assistant became the social barrier between Natalie and her peers. The children were being taught that Natalie was different and the staff were better equipped to be her friend. Staff can so quickly get in the way of true and simple connections.

To be clear, I totally agree that Natalie needed support in the classroom, but we still need to figure out how to support people while they pursue meaningful connection.

But wait! What if being a "Velcro staff" is what the community expects?

Unfortunately, we have taught people in the public that "we have got it" and staff should be attached to people twenty-four hours a day, seven days a week. This makes it hard as we try to support individuals to do a few things on their own. Often the community doesn't get what we are trying to achieve and may be concerned. We must educate community members too. Here are some examples of how to do that:

- When a waiter or waitress turns to a staff person and asks, "What does she want?" without acknowledging the person who is vulnerable standing there, you need to address this. Answer calmly but confidently, "Although I do help Jane with parts of her day, she does not need my help to order her food. Go ahead, Jane, and order. You got this!"

- When a doctor only looks at the staff and doesn't address the person who is there for the appointment. Physically stand and shift your body so you are looking at the person you support, not the doctor. If this doesn't help, you can again clarify your role. "Sorry, but I am just here to support Mike in a few areas of his life. You should talk directly to him."

- Just take things one event at a time and educate along the way. Keep in mind that inclusive-based supports may still be new to your organization, service provider, or community. This is not something we have been doing for 200 years! There is a learning curve for everyone.

A professional named Hilary told me a story about when she took Ed to the local pool. She realized that Ed could (and should) pay for his own pool fee. So, she handed him his five-dollar bill and he stood in line. Hilary waited at the other side of the entrance, giving him time and space to do this on his own (go Hilary!). When it was Ed's turn to pay, the cashier pointed and yelled towards Hilary in front of a busy lobby, "Hey, aren't you supposed to be here helping him do this? Isn't this your job?"

Yikes! How embarrassing for everyone! The community is going to struggle with what your job does and doesn't entail. I told Hilary to answer next time just as loudly but politely, like this:

"Yes, I support Ed in many parts of his life, but he doesn't need me to pay for him. Go ahead and pay, Ed, you got this." Then go back and debrief with your team. We need to support each other.

How do we begin to build up responsibility?

The question "What is one thing I do for someone that they could (and should) be doing for themselves?" is used in most of my speaking engagements. It is a safe question used within team meetings because it is not about requiring massive change, but about picking one small concept to work towards. Ideally, support teams should pick the same single goal to focus on. Maybe John can make his own toast? Mary can pick her own clothes? Martin can go to the bank on his own? Jo can plan the meals for Sunday night dinner?

Whatever it is, focus on just one thing and work collectively at supporting the people you care about to see if their skill develops or returns. Some people will flourish with this opportunity. Some people will be angry and frustrated. Go slowly and gently.

Once when I was attending a meeting in Jerry's house, his team struggled to think of anything he could do on his own. The great part of this meeting was that Jerry sat with us for the discussion. While he might not have understood all the conversation, his presence was so powerful.

I randomly asked if Jerry could get the mail from the mailbox. Suddenly, he jumped up and ran towards the door! The staff panicked. Was he bolting? Running away? Nope. He opened the door and got the mail from the mailbox. He returned to the kitchen table and plopped the mail down in front of us. Jerry's action quickly changed the conversation—in his own way he told us what interested him and showed us that he could do it! It ended up being an excellent meeting, and Jerry had real involvement in how he could be responsible for more at home. It was a moment I won't forget.

~~~~~~~~~~~~~~~~~~~~

Kristy was a young woman who was ready for more. During a team meeting that I attended, the staff agreed that Kristy could make the coffee for the house in the morning. A few months later, one of the team members called me with an update. Kristy was now making the coffee each morning, and that opportunity had led to her learning how to bake banana
~~~~~~~~~~~~~~~~~~~~

bread as well. That provided a further opportunity for Kristy to host her mom and aunt, which then led to her signing up to sell Tupperware. Amazing! Time and time again, people are so ready for more—more responsibility, more purpose, more quality moments within the day.

I hope that once we see the progress and conversations that can come from the gain (or relearning) of just one skill set, we will be encouraged to have further conversations. However, if something you try seems to be making a situation worse or making someone feel bad about themselves, then you are on the wrong path. Go back and try something else. Do not force something to continue for months (or years) that seems to be harming someone's self-esteem rather than helping it.

I was asked to meet with the team that supported Sarah. Sarah was thirty-five years old and the staff accurately felt she could, and should, use the toilet independently. When I was invited to join the meeting, they had been working on this skill for six months. It was not going well and Sarah was participating less and less in the things she liked because she was not following the goals and plans that the team had assigned her.

Let's be clear, I too think Sarah might have been able to have more independence in using the washroom, but this was no longer about learning skills. This was now a power struggle. In the end the washroom goals were all cancelled and Sarah went back to reconnecting with her community. It was time to move on.

Gaining a skill is not worth sacrificing quality social connection and community. Watch for power struggles! Remember, attaining responsibility should not negatively impact dignity and opportunities to build community.

Chapter 6 Let's apply this

HOW DO WE BUILD UP RESPONSIBILITY?

1. What are three things you will take away from reading this chapter? What can you apply right now?

2. How can you avoid becoming "Velcro staff"? How are you inadvertently getting in the way of people when they are trying to connect to their community?

3. What is one thing you do for people that they could do for themselves?

4. Think about how you are currently building dignity for the people you support. List what is working. What is the next step?

Chapter 7
What is the power of contribution?

Contribution is the loudest sign
that someone is being valued
and included.
—Cara Milne

Chapter 7

WHAT IS THE POWER OF CONTRIBUTION?

It is important that we support people to contribute to their homes and communities. This can be through big roles, like employment, or small moments, like putting napkins on the dinner table. There is no perfect answer here. It could be that someone contributes by taking out the garbage or walking a neighbour's dog. It could be something daily or maybe once a year. The value of contribution is not judged by how often it is done or how much money it earns, but how it builds dignity and self-esteem.

What are the ways that someone contributes?

So many great stories have come from this above question about contribution. Here are a few of my favourites.

Jenny and Brian have lived as roommates for over ten years. Every year the team supports them on a vacation a few hours away in the Okanagan. They have a great time! On the way home, they always stop and buy an enormous amount of fruit. Once home they keep a lot of the fruit for themselves, but also divide some up for their neighbours. The staff think that Jenny and Brian are more excited about delivering the fruit to their neighbours than about their actual vacation. Usually one of the neighbours turns around and bakes a pie for them. In the end, community can be created with such simple efforts.

~~~~~~~~~~~~~~~~~~~~

One of the day (vocational) programs I have worked with over the years is near some other businesses. On snowy days
~~~~~~~~~~~~~~~~~~~~

Eddy loves to shovel snow. The team takes the time to help him see which of these surrounding businesses need his help. As you can imagine, Eddy is a huge hit with all the different companies in the area. There have been intense conversations about whether Eddy should be paid for this, and I think for some people that would be a fantastic idea! However, for Eddy, money is not something he values. He does love a cup of coffee, so once a week he heads over to a different "shovel spot" and shares a coffee and treat with different business neighbours. These visits are not long, but they are perfect for him.

~~~~~~~~~~~~~~~~~~~~

Bailey had just moved to a new city and felt like she didn't have any social connections. Since Bailey didn't know where to start, the team helped her to connect with her local public library. She had attended adult colouring groups in her previous city and expressed a passion for colouring and connecting with others. With support from her team, Bailey connected with library staff and implemented a drop-in adult colouring group, which she named "Colouring Outside the Lines".

As I write this, Bailey has co-facilitated four drop-in sessions for adult colouring. She has united with others through common interests, exchanged telephone numbers, and gone for coffee and games with members of the group she created. I hope you get to have a Bailey at your local library too!

The fact is, there are more stories of people with disabilities having successful impact than I could possibly tell. Contribution is the loudest sign that someone is being valued
~~~~~~~~~~~~~~~~~~~~

and included. It is a good indicator, for example, that a child is on his way to be included in the classroom.

Everyone benefits

I have heard countless times how the presence of one child with a disability in a school has changed the entire culture of how all children learn and accept each other. Many people have shared with me that although they were supposed to be "helpers", they ended up receiving more than they gave. Where have you heard these kind of remarks? Often inclusive experiences end up completely changing peers, co-workers and neighbours.

Recently I was reminded that the value of contribution is not just an issue related to people with developmental disabilities. A dear friend Mike, who has spent his life loving and serving people as a pastor, husband, father, and friend, recently moved into a care facility due to Parkinson's disease. This has been devastating for his family, friends, and those who have been influenced by him.

His wife shared that as she visits him each day, she frequently finds him sitting alongside other residents. The staff say he is now the unofficial pastor at the facility! Even from his wheelchair, he is still able to sit beside people who seem lonely. He may not be able to talk clearly, and has lost so many skills, but he is **still** able to contribute. His presence is powerful!

Never doubt that every person has something to offer the world. Disability, age, poverty, or illness can often seem to limit someone's ability to influence our society. There is no influence too small. In fact, it seems over and over that the quietest and most vulnerable of voices create the loudest impact. All people can contribute.

Helping people find their own voice

Sometimes part of supporting people with disabilities is aiding them to explore their own voice and opinions. The human services field is trying to do this through organized groups, such as self-advocacy groups. They can be beneficial for all, and are a chance for people who are devalued to share ideas and opinions about how they wish they were supported and how the community needs to evolve so everyone can belong.

Here are a few thoughts when you are striving to help individuals find their own voice. Keep in mind that it is a process which will take time, energy, and dedication. We have been devaluing people for entire lifetimes—we cannot repair that overnight.

- **Aim to support mentors**. Mentors are people with disabilities who wish to share their own experiences and knowledge with others.

- **Aim to support social groups**. These groups provide opportunities for people with disabilities to plan and create events, helping individuals understand the different roles people play on a committee and how to work in a group or team. The key for this model is for staff to **back off**. Easier said than done.

- **Aim to support advocacy groups.** These differ from social groups, as they are not about planning the next party, but instead try to tackle bigger issues that affect the quality of life for people who are vulnerable. The process can take a long time, as you try to help people find their voice while they are still monitored by the staff who are paid to support them. Do you see the power struggle there? How can I tell you that my day is boring, when you are the person whom I must spend my days with? Here are a few things that might help:

    ✓ Have meetings away from the agency or facility (staff homes are a worse idea). Find a space that is still private (sorry, Tim Hortons is way too public). Often libraries or community centres have small boardrooms to rent. Or have someone in the group who has a disability host in their own home. Yes, this is going to be hard work to organize, but well worth the outcome.

    ✓ Make sure all language and information shared is written in **plain language**. Research this if it is unfamiliar for you. There are excellent organizations and resources that specialize in this subject.

    ✓ Help staff involved to understand what their role is and isn't. Pick one or two topics and focus on those in a quality way. Staff need specific training on how to be a support instead of a barrier.

- ✓ Don't give up. It is not going to happen right away. Treat the process with the respect the group deserves.

A great organization I know shared how it was thrilled when a letter came from its internal self-advocacy group. The letter outlined a few areas where people felt the organization was not meeting their needs. Imagine the bravery of the people who signed this letter! The voice of the people who actually receive services will always be the most powerful!

Whatever your organization is working towards, just keep going. It is not just about building up the voices and self-esteem for people who are devalued. It is important to note that government and funding bodies take very seriously the thoughts of families and individuals with disabilities. A letter written by staff is not as influential as a letter written by a family or self-advocate.

In the end, it will be people with disabilities that will finally steer us in the right direction. Let's make sure they are behind the steering wheel.

Chapter 7 Let's apply this

WHAT IS THE POWER OF CONTRIBUTION?

1. What are three things you will take away from reading this chapter? What can you apply right now?

2. a. Think of someone you support; how does that person with a disability contribute?

   b. What are the next steps? What needs to happen to deepen or continue this contribution?

   c. Share with your team a success story of how someone you support contributes to his or her community? Celebrate what is successful!

3. a. In what ways are people with disabilities finding their own voices?

   b. What can you do differently to treat this self-advocacy as important?

Chapter 8
What really matters? Relationships!

When relationships lead, skills will follow.

—Cara Milne

Chapter 8

WHAT REALLY MATTERS? RELATIONSHIPS!

What makes a good social support? Most people immediately think of their family, friends, or a significant other. While the answers are common, it is difficult to agree on how to create the bond itself. Staff need to understand the importance of searching for opportunities where the community can be a part of the social network for the individuals supported.

Natural supports

Friends, neighbours, church members, co-workers, and of course family members are all people we consider natural supports. They are not paid. Why is that important? While many staff have meaningful relationships with the people they care for, the reality is that staff members change. This means the relationship is both temporary and dependent upon employment. As a result, staff are not typically a permanent part of people's lives.

Consider someone you know with a disability. **How many staff do you think they have had within a year?** Their lifetime? What would that feel like?

This enquiry is one of my favourite questions to ask, especially when I know staff are willing to be honest and vulnerable. It reminds us that we are just one of hundreds of support staff who play a part in assisting each unique person. This conversation frequently makes students from my classrooms cry. Why? I think it reminds them that the "great" work we may have done as teams could have left a family vulnerable or lost.

Respecting families

Professionals don't always know best. Sorry. I know that is hard to hear. There are some outstanding support staff who are literally changing lives as I type this. However, professionals make mistakes. We make large and small decisions that derail and often ignore the voice of families and individuals.

I always say that the best education I could have ever asked for was to be part of a parent-led advocacy organization for over ten years. I was a front-row student listening to families and their stories. I was forced to see my work through the lens of a mom or dad. I witnessed the role professionals can play as guests in people's lives. Whether they are there short term or long term, **staff are rarely permanent**. I am forever grateful for learning this lesson early in my career.

I can't tell you how many times in my travels I have heard about "difficult guardians". Please stop using this term. Parents who want the very best for their children who have disabilities are much more than guardians and have an absolute right to be difficult. As professionals, we must begin to see and respect the experience of parents before they arrive at our office. Everyone in the partnership will be better if we start there.

Act like a guest, and I guarantee the journey working alongside families will be better!

I sometimes tell my story about Margeaux, whom I was supporting to find a job. She was an energetic and bright twenty-three-year-old woman with a developmental disability. We hit it off instantly! I quickly helped her find a job, but she needed to take the bus to get to work. She then told me she was not allowed to take the bus. What? I figured it was her parents being overprotective, and so I wrote home (no email at that time). My letter explained **my goals** for Margeaux and how I thought she was totally capable of learning this new skill. Her parents' response was . . . no. I figured the family was being very "difficult" and not seeing Margeaux as the capable young adult whom I saw.

Not long after, I was in a face-to-face meeting with Mom. She was a lovely lady and brought up the issue of taking transit. She then chose to share their family story with me: when Margeaux was younger, she would often take the bus home from school, until a group of girls repeatedly beat her up on the bus, followed her home, and threatened her. They were horrible and cruel.

I have been humbled so many times in my career, but that moment will always be painful and fresh. I thought I knew best. Yet I didn't have a clue about what this family had experienced before I became involved. Once I really listened and respected the family, we quickly found a better solution—a job for Margeaux that was much closer to home. No transit needed.

When working alongside families, keep in mind that they are the primary and often most important natural support for the people you care about.

A shift in thinking about support

I think we need to look at supports differently. We have been too focused on the individual and missed looking for the community. We need to watch for the ever-possible connections that surround everyone with a disability whom we support. In the past, we have focused only on a person's interest, abilities, and goals. My challenge is to move away from a model that only focuses on the person,

and change it to this!

As you can see from my awesome drawing, the team not only focuses on the person, but also provides a greater awareness of the potential of the surrounding community. This shift in perspective considers the person **and** an awareness of who surrounds the person to become part of their support system. It may just be someone they will wave to at the store. Community is everywhere. Let's focus on reducing isolation!

A great agency I have worked with told me a story of how Ronnie, who had recently moved, needed to learn the new bus route to his favourite pool hall. One of the friends he knew from the pool hall ended up providing some natural support, including navigating the schedule and even helping with bus training. Ronnie can now get there independently, but more importantly, the team slowed down and invited someone from the community to help. Keep taking the time to see who is interested in being involved.

What does this look like in practice? It means that, for example, not only do I go with Steve to the gym, but I am also aware of who else is at the gym who seems to be interested in or friendly towards Steve. It may be that Steve (once reminded and supported) will be able to have a good conversation on his own. Or it may be that I need to pursue the conversation with a potential new contact. I could say, "Did you know Steve likes the Stampeders too?" or "Did you know Steve has been coming here for two years?" Of course, this may not always work, but it might. The key is being brave and aware to help create opportunities. Once we are aware of the possible community that exists for people, we can aim to pursue it and see where it leads.

Staff are facilitators of pursuing and increasing social opportunities. Professionals can often best serve people with disabilities by taking the time to get to know their possible social connections. Who is in their life? Who is missing? This never-ending, important journey can begin to reduce the risks of isolation and loneliness.

Who is a possible social connection?

Social connections include a variety of relationships. Frequently, there is a focus only on "friends", but it is important to acknowledge that there can be all types of influences that lead to a sense of belonging.

- **Family relationships** include parents, siblings, and extended family.

- **Customer relationships** are with people we pay for services and are an important connection—our hairdresser, childcare provider, support team, or doctor, for example.

- **Membership relationships** exist in places we attend regularly based on the roles we have. This is often where our name is written down somewhere—our gym, team, school, workplace, photography class, sewing club, or church, for example.

- **Community relationships** are with the people we are connected to as we journey—our neighbours, the folks on the bus route, or the other parents from our children's school, for example.

- **Friend relationships** develop with people whom we have met repeatedly due to roles in life, but now we are connected because they care about and are interested in our life. We are hopefully a good friend in return.

I recently heard a story about a lovely lady named Brianna, whom Andrea supported. Brianna and Andrea often went to the same coffee shop, and Andrea noticed that Brianna and the barista always chatted and totally hit it off. Unfortunately, Brianna passed away. A few months later, Andrea was back at the coffee shop and the barista asked where Brianna was. When Andrea said that Brianna had passed away, the barista started to cry. She was devastated and shared that she wished she had known, and would have liked to have attended the funeral.

When Andrea told me this story, she became emotional. She had not realized the depth of the simple relationship that had developed at the coffee shop. Andrea regretted not taking the time to support it—and yet it was a beautiful legacy of the impact Brianna had on the world. Relationships can be anywhere.

When relationships lead, skills will follow

One last thing we should keep in mind: it is important to not always place skill development before relationships. I have seen children in schools being taught hours of communication skills alone with a teacher's assistant. Why not connect that child with other kids the same age and then try to apply language skills? Although there may be a need for very short and specific isolated skill development in schools (or in adult learning), too often people are secluded to learn these skills. We tend to support children to learn skills in order to talk with friends, when we should be supporting children to have relationships and practice skills **with** their friends.

Some of my personal stories are harder to tell than others. Many years ago, I supported a little boy named Matt. He was nine years old and an amazing kid. We spent a lot of time together every day after school, and I was there to give his parents a break (respite) and help him learn skills. I worked with Matt for nine months. Ask me how many times I helped that great kid play with anyone else his own age? Any guesses? Yep, you guessed it—**never**. I never once thought about the fact that I was his only playmate. It is heartbreaking every time I tell that story. Yet I know it propels me to build communities for others.

I wish I could tell a different story. I could have at least tried different options! Maybe there was someone his age at the park? Maybe we could have invited someone over from next door? Maybe . . . but I never even made the effort. In hindsight, I believed that I was all he needed. I was very wrong. I worked with him for nine months straight and then I left and took a different job. He ended up more alone than when I got there.

It is in telling this story that I summarize this chapter. If I had recognized that I was just a guest in Matt's life, I would have hopefully looked for others who could have been a permanent part of Matt's life. I would have helped him build community via my support. I would have spent time not only building his skills but also helping him practice those skills with others. I was supposed to be helping him with communication; too bad he had no friends to talk to.

I wish I had left a different legacy.

Chapter 8 Let's apply this

WHAT REALLY MATTERS? RELATIONSHIPS!

1. What are three things you will take away from reading this chapter? What can you apply right now?

2. Where are natural supports for the people you care about? List them and ways to further build up their connections.

3. What stories have families taught you that have changed the direction of your work?

4. How are you building up relationships? Be creative in looking for all kinds of connection possibilities!

5. When reflecting on, as support staff, you are often “just a guest”, what comes to your mind?

6. Dream about what legacy you wish to leave behind when you consider the people you are currently supporting.

7. What do you need to do to leave a legacy of **community building** versus **isolation**?

Chapter 9
Where do we begin?

It is never about big change, but starting with small and meaningful actions. Just start where you are!
—Cara Milne

Chapter 9

WHERE DO WE BEGIN?

I am frequently asked to provide some key topics or areas that would be most helpful when an opportunity arises to educate a community group. Churches (including Sunday schools, youth groups, and congregations), youth services (playgroups, Brownies, Scouts, etc.), and many sports teams are often willing or interested in having some training or information when supporting people with disabilities. The public wants to help—people just need to know where to begin. In the end, any respectful conversation with a community group is a start. Below are just a few ideas.

Language

Talk to teams or groups about using person-first language. Remember to always refer to **people with disabilities**, not "disabled people".

Tone of voice

Prompt the public to not talk to adults with disabilities like they are babies. For example, avoid using a high-pitched and condescending tone of voice.

Respect

Remind the public that children or adults are more than their disability. I regularly tell community groups to presume competence, meaning that they should assume that a person who is vulnerable can understand everything they are saying. That doesn't mean we don't provide support or meet needs.

However, when starting a conversation with an adult who has a disability whom you don't know, talk to him or her as you would any other person. More often than not, when we go in with high expectations, those expectations will be met.

Space

Remind the community group that a support person or volunteer should not take over everything. It is important to be upfront about not wanting to become "Velcro staff" and take over all aspects of that person's care. This is such an important discussion to have. For example, a Sunday school class might want to include Jessica, but assume that her volunteer will do everything for her.

When I offer training to teams or groups, I remind them of the importance of having Jessica connect to her peers. We need to focus **on relationships first** and skills or academics second. In this way, the teacher knows that even when I am not always next to Jessica, I am still doing my job.

Contribution

Explain that nobody wants to be a charity and everyone wants a chance to participate and contribute to the larger group. I encourage you to help community organizations understand that it is not just about Mike attending youth group, for example, but also about giving him a valuable yet fitting role. Other kids have roles; Mike should have one too, and not just a "special job". If everyone is bringing soup for a fundraiser, so should he.

Roles

Make sure you talk about who the people with disabilities are beyond their labels. What interests them? How are they similar to their peers? What are their roles and interests?

> Some stories come as a gift. A week before I was to send this book to be printed, I received an email from a friend's music teacher. It was such a perfect example of everything I teach. This is exactly what it said:
>
> "This year we have invited John, Stephanie's brother, as our special guest to our Christmas concert. John has been working very hard for the past couple of years to learn to play the piano. Stephanie wanted to make you aware prior to the concert that John has autism and will sometimes make involuntary noises that can be a bit distracting. Along with playing the piano, John is most excited about having an event to which he can wear a bow tie. If you would like to chat with him after the concert, John loves sports, trains, rock climbing, and piano, and enjoys talking about them. I am sure you will join me in welcoming him for this concert."
>
> Honestly, this email gives me hope.

Questions

Give time for people to ask real and honest questions. This is where you will regularly break down the most stereotypes. If you can reassure the Sunday school teachers that, no, the child in their class is not aggressive, you are breaking down stereotypes. When we give a chance for the community to ask questions, we also need to respond patiently. No one wants to feel ignorant and embarrassed.

I enjoy helping church congregations and other community groups that are including people who are vulnerable. Often just listening to questions and helping break down preconceptions are more powerful than any lecture or training I could offer. Keep educating people, one quality conversation and one question at a time.

Rebecca's story

As a final story in this book, I have included an experience that I hope will help show the variety of issues, questions, and outcomes that are possible when we take things slowly and focus on relationships.

Many years ago, I was asked to help Rebecca attend Sunday school. All I knew was that Rebecca was a little girl who loved dolls, didn't verbally communicate, and had never been to a church before. It is important to acknowledge here that having more information about her diagnosis really would not have been helpful. Beyond allergies and major triggers, I just needed to get to know Rebecca.

The first few weeks did not go well, and there were many tears (from Rebecca, me, and her mom too!). I continued to tell her mom that we would just keep trying. I could not promise that Rebecca would love Sunday school or that she would be included. However, I could promise that there were volunteers who were willing to keep trying. (I believe that when we work with families, we shouldn't make promises we can't keep.)

Finally, after months of effort, Rebecca's situation got better. A team was formed, where volunteers could ask questions and learn about Rebecca. Stereotypes came down.

Rebecca had a wonderful sense of humour and showed her abilities more each week. She spent most of her time with her own same-aged class, but would occasionally need to take a walk around with just a volunteer. It was not perfect and some weeks were messy; she would bolt, cry, or not want to connect to anyone at all. However, one wise team member reminded me that until that year, Rebecca's mom had not been able to attend church at all. **We were doing work that mattered**, even if some weeks it wasn't as inclusive or successful as I wanted it to be.

A glimpse into the details

Below are a few questions we considered that helped us get on the right track with Rebecca. To be clear, the following decisions worked for her. **They may not work for someone else**. It is not always possible to find perfect answers, but keep asking the critical questions that could best help children and adults successfully belong in their community.

- Should Rebecca be placed with children five years younger than her? Our answer was no, she should be with her same-aged peers.

- Should Rebecca be one-on-one with a volunteer the entire time and learn alone in a separate classroom? Although this would have been easier, our answer was no, everyone else would miss out on getting to know her.

- Should we have a few volunteers who rotate each week? Our answer was yes, having more than one person connected to Rebecca would help her build relationships and not rely on just one person. It would also prevent volunteer burnout.

- Should we should move more of the dolls into her grade 6 classroom? Rebecca had a few with her for comfort, but I was considering moving the larger doll toys too. Our answer was no. In truth, I was not sure on this one, so I asked the other kids in the class. They rolled their eyes and said that the dolls should stay in the kindergarten class. I thought they were pretty wise.

- Should we change the format of the lesson to include more physical playtime, more snack breaks, and more movement? Our answer was **yes**! Once the format was changed, all the other kids flourished too. We all benefit when we all belong.

So how did we build in contribution? Rebecca handed out the craft materials and supplies, just like everyone else. It was a work in progress! On the flip side, we noticed a couple of the girls in the class loved helping Rebecca when she was struggling. So, instead of the volunteer doing everything, we asked her peers if they wanted to help. They did! Please, please celebrate when these little moments happen. When a peer from a soccer team or a friend from Scouts steps up and is willing to help, celebrate! It is a priceless difference maker.

The family eventually moved away. I think it was a loss for that grade and, in fact, the entire church. Those kids and many adults were learning so much about patience, respect, and what it meant to include someone. We were all becoming better.

Where are these kinds of opportunities in your community? School? Sports teams? Neighbourhoods? Go! Go! Go!

Cara's Top 10 for building community

I am going to leave you with my Top 10 list. These recommendations represent some of the concepts that I consider the most significant and which have become, in essence, the guiding principles of my work. My experiences have shown me over and over that community building is never about big change but about small and meaningful actions.

1. Keep in mind that you are the arms, legs, and voices for people. You can either build up stereotypes or tear them down.

2. Slow down! Take the time to look and see the community that is everywhere.

3. Recognize that quality roles with a focus on purpose are way more important than filling time and just keeping busy.

4. Celebrate! Be proud of the small but significant steps towards inclusive practice. Tell stories of the real successes that happen every day.

5. Focus on building up dignity and self-esteem by supporting people to contribute and have responsibility!

6. Get out of the way! Make sure you aren't preventing people from building meaningful communities of their own.

7. Listen to the stories of families and individuals with disabilities. They will guide you in the right direction.

8. Remember that you are a valuable guest in people's lives. What will your legacy be?

9. Wave at the neighbours!

10. Consider what matters most. It really is the people around us. It's having valuable and purposeful things to do in the day. It's feeling valued and respected. It's belonging!

My final thoughts

There are so many more stories and examples that I would have loved to share with you. In the end my hope is that my passion has shone through. Through this writing process, I have become even more convicted of what I know to be true: building communities is for everyone. It is not and never has been just for people who are vulnerable. When all people have opportunities to contribute and feel valued, we can say we are truly building community.

We are better together.

Have feedback or want more information?
Contact Cara Milne of M-Powered Planning Ltd. at
www.mpoweredplanning.com

Acknowledgements

A THOUSAND WAYS I AM THANKFUL

There are so many people who have contributed to the stories in this book. So, I will start way back at the beginning. Thank you to Dr. Shelley Kinash, who saw something in me long before I saw it in myself. To Debbie Baggs and Sue Huffman, who taught me how to teach, I sure miss working with both of you. To the amazing people I have worked alongside over the years, I am better because of you! Thank you to the Lethbridge Association for Community Living, and the families who taught me more than any post-secondary education could.

Thank you to my own communities of friends, who have loved me and supported me as a professional, mom, and friend. To Erin, Nicole, and the other amazing Lethbridge women whom I raised my babies with, I survived with joy because of you. To the wise women I share Tuesday mornings with, you have forever changed me and my faith. To the people I get to share my neighbourhood (and book pub) with, my family will never be able to move homes because of all of you. To the families in Calgary that I currently raise my girls alongside, I have no words to describe how much I enjoy being on this exiting adventure with you. We have an amazing village!

Monika, you are the best carpool mom and friend I could have asked for. Leanne, I don't think I could put one foot in front of the other if it wasn't for our friendship. You are the reason this work happens! Shannon Wiebe, you are a gift that I am thankful for daily. Kristin and Amy, I have learned the joy of community from our lifetime together.

I have a community of family members who are strong, loud, amazing, and a tad dysfunctional—they are perfect! Thank you to my mom, dad, and my brother, Curtis, who taught me early on how to really love people. Thank you to my bonus family of Penny and Bree. Thank you to my Milne family, who have included me from the beginning and, now that I have written this, will allow me to talk even more at Christmas.

I send a huge thank you to John Paul Yoos, Tricia Wheatley, and Corey Hadden for slogging through the first draft of this book and making it so much better. Thank you to the amazing and talented Jaime Miller for making all these words shine! Thank you to the Reitsma family, John, Angela, Bailey, and the team at Saskatchewan Abilities Council Regina, who helped me tell some great new stories.

And finally, I am thankful for my amazing blue-eyed boy, who is the best friend and partner anyone could ask for. Darren, home will always be where you are. I love you!

I could write another entire chapter on my love and thankfulness for my girls, Jaden and Ashley. I love being your mom. You inspire me daily. I can't wait to see how you change the world!

And last, with praise to my precious Lord Jesus, I can do all things through Him who strengthens me.

Wishing you all good things,

Cara

Notes:

Ideas:

Goals:_

References

Angelou, Maya. January 16, 2011. *Oprah's Master Class*. http://www.oprah.com/own-master-class/Dr-Maya-Angelou-on-the-Power-of-Words-Video.

Damour, Lisa. 2016. *Untangled: Guiding Teenage Girls through the Seven Transitions into Adulthood*. New York: Ballantine Books.

Government of Alberta Human Services. 2016. *Persons with Developmental Disabilities (PDD) Program: Abuse Prevention and Response Protocol (APRP) Training Manual*. http://www.humanservices.alberta.ca/pdd-online/documents/abuse-prevention-and-response-protocol-training-manual.pdf.

Pinker, Susan. 2014. *The Village Effect: How Face-to-Face Contact Can Make Us Healthier and Happier*. Toronto: Random House Canada.

Snow, Kathie. 2008. "A Few Words about People First Language." https://www.disabilityisnatural.com/pfl-articles.html.